Patrick Hickey

Raoul Wallenberg
Swedish Diplomat
and Humanitarian

Thomas Streissguth

THE ROSEN PUBLISHING GROUP, INC.
NEW YORK

Published in 2001 by The Rosen Publishing Group, Inc.
29 East 21st Street, New York, NY 10010

First Edition

Library of Congress Cataloging-in-Publication Data

Streissguth, Thomas, 1958–
    Raoul Wallenberg : Swedish diplomat and humanitarian / by Tom Streissguth — 1st ed.
            p. cm. — (Holocaust biographies)
Includes bibliographical references (p.   ) and index
    ISBN 0-8239-3318-0 (lib. binding)
    1. Wallenberg, Raoul—Juvenile literature. 2. Righteous Gentiles in the Holocaust—Biography—Juvenile literature 3. Diplomats—Sweden—Biography—Juvenile literature. 4. World War, 1939–1945—Jews—Rescue—Hungary—Juvenile literature 5. Holocaust, Jewish (1939–1945)—Hungary—Juvenile literature. 6. Hungary—Ethnic relations—Juvenile literature. [1. Wallenberg, Raoul 2. Diplomats 3. Jews—Hungary 4. Holocaust, Jewish (1939–1945)—Hungary 5. World War, 1939–1945—Jews—Rescue.] I. Title. II. Series.
    D804.66.W35 S77 2000
    940.54'77943912'092—dc21
                                                                00-009892

Manufactured in the United States of America

Contents

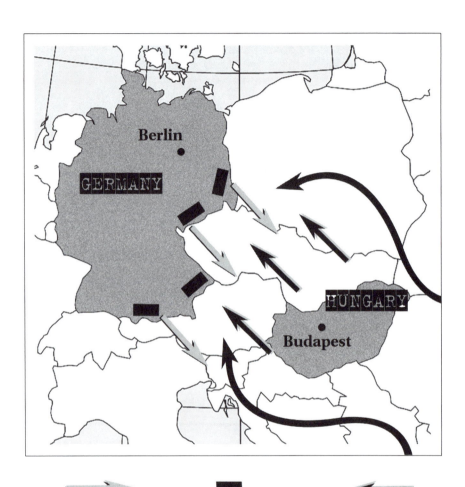

Berlin

GERMANY

HUNGARY

Budapest

German
counterattack

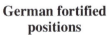

German fortified
positions

Soviet
armored thrust

1. A Restless Banker

Angry guards shoved the frightened men toward the open doors of a cattle train. The train's engineer fired his locomotive, sending swirls of black smoke up and down the platform. The shouts of the guards mixed with the sound of gunfire and the barking of dogs. Hearing the dogs and seeing the rifles and machine guns, the men stumbled away from them, into the dark freight cars. Sliding doors closed behind them. Bolts and fasteners moved into place with a loud, heavy clatter.

Within a few minutes, hundreds of men were locked in the train. There were eighty men to each car. They stood shoulder to shoulder. There was no food and no place to sit or lie down. It was November 29, 1944, a busy day at the Josef Varos station in Budapest, Hungary.

November 1944: Raoul Wallenberg *(on the right, with his hands clasped)* provides protective Swedish passports to Jewish deportees at the Josef Varos train station in Budapest, Hungary.

The operation went smoothly. The guards were sending away a trainload of Jewish workers. The workers would travel to Austria. There they would build trenches to help German troops fighting against the armies of the Soviet Union. When the work was finished, the workers would be sent to a concentration camp. There they would be murdered.

Standing nearby and closely watching the train were officers of Germany's *Schutzstaffel*, or SS. Their commander, Adolf Eichmann, had arranged for this train. Eichmann was determined to murder every last Jew in Hungary. He had already sent half a million Jews out of the country to death camps in Poland and Germany. There were few Hungarians willing or able to stop him.

One of the officers saw a man dressed in a civilian coat and hat run along the platform toward him. The man was waving his arms, yelling, and cursing. The officer drew himself up. He pulled out his revolver. He placed it just inches from the man's stomach. The civilian grew angrier. He began jumping up and down and screaming. Although he was a Swede, he spoke perfect German. He ordered the officer to stop the operation immediately.

Guards and prisoners watched the strange argument. Nervous and unsure of what to do, the SS officer put his gun away. The man in civilian clothes quickly moved away. He walked up and down alongside the train. He barked orders at the men on the platform and at the men aboard the train. He asked for papers—everybody must show their papers. All those with papers must get off the train immediately.

The prisoners searched their pockets. They pulled out passes, certificates, bills, scraps, any piece of paper with printing on it. The civilian sat down at a table, pulling the men away from the train with his loud, commanding voice. He pulled out blank papers of his own, signed them quickly, and handed them out. He pointed toward a line of trucks waiting outside the station. Three hundred men climbed into the trucks.

Raoul Wallenberg, a member of a prominent Swedish family, was born in 1912.

The civilian left. He had just tricked the SS officer into sparing the lives of 300 men. He had been doing the same for almost five months in this dangerous and violent place far from his home.

Growing Up Swedish

Raoul Gustav Wallenberg was born on August 4, 1912. His father, also named Raoul Wallenberg, had served as an officer in the Swedish navy. But Raoul Wallenberg Sr. would never see the infant who carried on his name. The elder Wallenberg died of cancer in May 1912. It was just three months before the birth of his son and eight months after his marriage to Maj Wising.

Everybody in Sweden knew the name of Wallenberg. Members of this wealthy and important family had been bankers, business-men, military officers, government ministers, and diplomats. At the time of Raoul Wallenberg's birth, his grandfather, Gustav Wallenberg, was Sweden's ambassador to Japan.

In 1918, Maj Wallenberg remarried. Her second husband, Fredrik von Dardel, worked in Sweden's Ministry of Health. Maj and Fredrik von Dardel had two children, Guy and Nina. They were the younger half brother and half sister of Raoul Wallenberg.

Raoul Wallenberg enjoyed a happy child-hood. His mother and stepfather watched over him. His grandfather looked after his education. Raoul attended good schools and had many friends. But with the name Wallenberg also came responsibility. Gustav Wallenberg wanted his grandson to become a businessman or a banker. The Wallenbergs owned the Enskilda Bank and Gustav expected Raoul to work at this bank. Gustav also had the idea to set up an international Wallenberg bank someday. If Raoul proved himself, he might become the president of this bank.

Raoul had other ideas. Buildings interested him much more than money or banking. He spent long hours at construction sites, watching the work in progress. He learned everything he could about architecture. He read many books about how buildings were designed and built.

After high school, Raoul spent nine months in the military. (All Swedish men had to perform military service after finishing school.) Gustav then arranged for Raoul to travel to and live in foreign countries. He knew that many Swedes never traveled and he wanted something different for his grandson: the experience of foreign cultures and foreign languages.

In 1931, Raoul Wallenberg left for the United States. There he enrolled at the University of Michigan, in the city of Ann Arbor. He studied his favorite subject, architecture. He finished his course after just three and a half years. For his good work, Raoul won a school prize.

Raoul did not live in Ann Arbor the whole time he was in America. He traveled all over the western United States and toured Mexico. In the summer of 1933, he worked at the Chicago World's Fair. Raoul worked at the Swedish pavilion.

Raoul often hitchhiked, standing along the highways and asking strangers for rides. He was young and didn't worry much about the dangers of hitchhiking. Once, while returning to Ann Arbor from Chicago, he was picked up by four men in a car. Soon afterward, the men drove off the main road and onto a dirt lane. There they robbed Raoul at gunpoint.

Raoul was carrying very little money. But instead of panicking, he calmly asked the thieves for a ride back to the highway. They

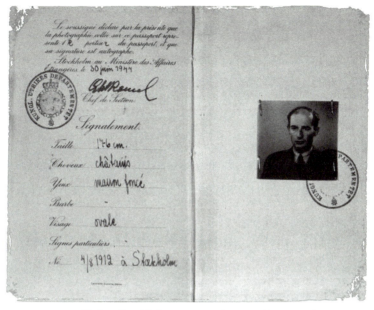

This Swedish passport was issued to Raoul Wallenberg in 1944. A restless young man, Wallenberg traveled extensively.

agreed at first. But his coolness made them so nervous they soon changed their minds. They dumped him in a ditch and fled the scene.

The robbers didn't harm Raoul Wallenberg, but they did teach Raoul an important lesson. He didn't always need a weapon or physical strength to face an enemy. Sometimes a strong voice and self-confidence were all that he needed.

Travel, Work, and Frustration

After returning to Sweden, Raoul prepared to settle down. He would follow the career that his grandfather had prepared for him—he would become a serious businessman. Gustav Wallenberg still wanted Raoul to see the world and to meet as many different people as possible. In 1935, he sent Raoul to Cape Town, South Africa. There Raoul worked as a traveling salesman for the Swedish South African Export/Import Company. He met architects, engineers, and builders. He sold construction materials, and he did well at it. But he earned no money in this job. He was still just a trainee.

Raoul's frustration grew. After six months, his grandfather arranged another position for him, a job in the Holland Bank. The bank had one of its branches in Haifa, a port city in Palestine. Again, Raoul worked without pay. In Haifa, Wallenberg stayed in a boarding house where he met Jewish families who had moved to

Palestine from Europe. Many of these Jews were escaping Germany. In 1933, the Nazi Party had taken power in Germany. Following the ideas of Adolf Hitler, their leader, the Nazis passed laws to control or harm the Jewish population. Hitler hated the Jews and blamed them for Germany's defeat in World War I in 1918.

The new laws forced many German Jews to leave their homes and their businesses. Fearing even worse persecution, thousands of Jews fled the country. Others remained behind. They thought the troubles would pass and that they would survive. They couldn't yet imagine that Hitler and the Nazis were planning to destroy the Jews completely.

Career Choices

In Haifa, Raoul worked hard. But he soon realized that he would make a poor banker. He found the banker's life very boring. He didn't like spending his days handling money. He didn't like dealing with the bank's many

When Adolf Hitler's Nazi Party came to power
in Germany in 1933, thousands of German Jews
fled the country to avoid persecution.

rules and regulations. He didn't like turning down people who wanted to borrow money. Instead, he wanted to help people, somehow.

In 1937, Gustav Wallenberg died. Without his grandfather's guidance, Raoul Wallenberg felt unsure of what to do. He went into business but failed. He offered designs for buildings and parks in Stockholm, but these projects never left his drawing board. In the fall of 1939, while he was still trying to find his career, Raoul heard the news that Germany had attacked Poland. Great Britain and France then declared war on Germany. World War II had begun. The war put an end to Raoul's plans of becoming an architect. All new construction stopped in Sweden and throughout Europe. The war also prevented Raoul from traveling freely, as he once had, on the European continent.

In the spring of 1940, the Nazi armies marched into France, the Netherlands, and Belgium. France surrendered, and German troops marched into Paris, the French capital. Wherever they went, the Nazis began passing

Germany invaded Poland in the
fall of 1939.

new laws against the Jews. They marked Jewish homes and forced Jews to wear yellow stars to identify themselves. Members of the SS arrived in German-occupied territory. They arrested, beat, tortured, and murdered Jews wherever they went.

Sweden remained neutral during World War II. The Swedish government did not ally itself with Germany or with Germany's enemies. Because they were neutral, Swedish diplomats could travel anywhere and meet with the leaders of any nation. The Swedes considered their territory, and their people, to be safe from attack and arrest.

After the war began, Raoul Wallenberg met Koloman Lauer, a Jewish businessman. Lauer had left Hungary, his native land, and moved to Sweden. Hungary had allied itself with Nazi Germany, and the Hungarian leaders had passed new anti-Jewish laws of their own. These laws made it impossible for Lauer to stay in Hungary and carry on his business. Lauer's business was the Central European

The Nazis spread their hatred of the Jews
throughout Europe. In Hungary and elsewhere, Jews
were forced to wear badges to identify themselves.

Trading Company. This firm bought and sold food and dry goods in Sweden and the rest of Europe. Because he could no longer travel in much of Europe, Lauer hired Raoul Wallenberg as a salesman. Wallenberg's job would be to travel all over the continent for the company.

Raoul Wallenberg eagerly accepted the new position. Finally he had found something that suited him well. He loved to travel, and he loved to make deals. He had a gift for languages—he could speak French, German, English, and Russian fluently. He had a knack for sizing up people, for understanding their characters, and for learning what they wanted. He had a friendly, enthusiastic manner and a lot of energy. All these qualities made him an ideal salesman for Koloman Lauer.

Hungarian fascists formed the Nyilas, or Arrow
Cross, in imitation of Germany's Nazi Party.

2. A Swedish Diplomat in Hungary

As a salesman for the Central European Trading Company, Wallenberg first traveled to Paris in late 1941. By this time, German troops were occupying the city. They strictly controlled people arriving or leaving. As a neutral Swede and a businessman, Wallenberg could move around freely. He also traveled to Germany and to Hungary, Lauer's native land. In Budapest, Wallenberg spent several weeks meeting people, doing business, and walking in the streets. He also visited Koloman Lauer's family to make sure they were safe.

Hungary had allied itself with Nazi Germany, but it also had one of the largest communities of Jews in Europe. Before the war, there had been 400,000 Jews living in Hungary. About half of them lived in the Hungarian capital of Budapest. The Jews had been living in Hungary for more than one thousand years. They made up an important part of Hungarian society. Many of Hungary's lawyers, doctors, merchants, and business owners were Jewish. There were Jewish teachers, artists, writers, and musicians.

Most of the Christian Hungarians accepted the Jewish people who lived among them. Yet Hungary also had an anti-Semitic streak. Some Hungarians saw the Jews as foreigners, even as enemies. In imitation of Germany's Nazi Party, Hungarian anti-Semites formed the Nyilas, or Arrow Cross. The Arrow Cross had its own uniforms, flags, and symbol—a pair of crossed arrows. But unlike the Nazi Party, the Arrow Cross had won no elections. The leaders of the Arrow Cross had not succeeded in taking power.

While traveling in Europe, Raoul Wallenberg had his first experience of life under Nazi occupation. Wherever German armies had conquered, German officers and troops marched confidently through the streets. The Germans wore the swastika, the symbol of Hitler's Nazi Party, and flew Nazi flags from important government buildings. They set curfews at night, closed down businesses, and arrested people for violating curfew and other rules. German SS troops broke into homes and rounded up Jewish families. They sent their prisoners to concentration camps in the countryside.

In Germany, Wallenberg saw many frightened Jews. Some were still trying to flee the country. But since the start of the war, the Jews had been trapped. They could not leave Germany. They could not even leave their own homes, except for a few hours a day. They were forbidden to run businesses or attend religious services in their synagogues. Their children could not go to school.

These sights deeply affected Raoul Wallenberg. He realized that he was doing nothing to

Wallenberg's travels in Nazi-occupied Europe made him want to fight the Nazis. Here, residents of Ober-Ramstadt, Germany, watch as a synagogue is destroyed by fire.

help. He felt a strong sympathy for the Jews suffering persecution under the Nazis. His own great-great-grandfather, Michael Benediks, had been one of the first Jews to settle in Sweden. Wallenberg was proud of his own Jewish blood. He began to feel frustrated with his business and his carefree life. With the coming of the war, there seemed much more important things to do. He imagined himself rescuing people, protecting them from harm or even death, and helping them to escape. Somehow and somewhere, he wanted to fight the Nazis.

An Occupied Country

On March 18, 1944, German troops marched into Hungary. There was no fighting, as Hungary and Germany were still allies. But the Germans soon let everybody know who was in charge. German troops patrolled the streets and country roads. German tanks and artillery maneuvered in the outskirts of

Budapest. Dome Sztojay, who was friendly with the Germans, became the prime minister. Germany ruled Hungary through its own ministers and diplomats. These officials arrived in Budapest to give the Hungarian government instructions straight from Adolf Hitler.

German SS units went about their work in Hungarian towns and villages. Between March and July 1944, these units deported 230,000 Jews from Hungary. They loaded their prisoners on freight trains and shipped them across Hungary's border with Poland. After several days, the trains arrived at Auschwitz. At this camp, prison guards killed thousands of Jews every day by poisoning them with gas. The bodies were burned in large ovens. Auschwitz became a factory of death.

The Nazis had laid out plans to make all of Europe *Judenrein,* or "free of Jews." They had almost succeeded in France, the Netherlands, Poland, and other nations they had conquered. The majority of Jews living in

Jews await deportation at an
assembly point.

these areas were now dead or imprisoned.
Hungary represented the last obstacle to this
goal. During the first four years of the war,
Hungary had been a haven for Jews, even
though Hungary had aligned with Germany.
Jews from Romania, Czechoslovakia, and
Poland had come in search of a safe place to
live. Germany had demanded that Hungary
deport its Jews and send them to the death

Adolf Eichmann was sent to
Hungary to eliminate the Jews.

camps. But until March 1944, the leaders of Hungary had refused to cooperate.

Hungary had passed many new laws against the Jews, however. Jews were forced to sell farmland they owned. They were segregated from Christians at public events. Most could no longer obtain licenses to become doctors or lawyers. And those Jews who arrived in Hungary seeking a safe haven from the Nazis found that not even Hungary was safe. The Hungarian government allowed the Germans to send foreign non-Hungarian Jews to their deaths in Auschwitz.

For the task of making Hungary *Judenrein*, Germany sent Adolf Eichmann. Eichmann was a lieutenant colonel in the SS. For two years, he had been rounding up Jewish civilians, placing them on packed freight trains, and shipping them to concentration camps. Eichmann had destroyed Jewish communities in Austria, Germany, France, and Czechoslovakia. He hated Jews with a passion and felt proud of his accomplishments. In the spring of 1944, he turned to Hungary.

By the summer, Eichmann had finished his task in the Hungarian countryside. But there were still 175,000 Jews living in Budapest. It was the last large community of Jews left in Nazi-occupied Europe. Eichmann was confident that he could make Budapest *Judenrein*. But he knew there was no time to waste. The armies of the Soviet Union were pushing back German units on the eastern front. In June 1944, the Allies—led by the United States—invaded northern France. Germany, as Eichmann and everyone else realized, was losing the war.

The War Refugee Board

In the United States, President Franklin Roosevelt and other government officials knew about the Nazi persecution of Jews in Europe. Reports had revealed that the Germans were forcing Jews out of their homes and putting them in concentration camps. The Germans were also setting up labor camps, where Jewish prisoners worked as slaves.

The United States had entered the war in December 1941. But for more than two years, the United States. and the Allies did very little to stop the Nazi campaign against the Jews. There seemed more important goals to achieve, such as defeating Germany and its ally, Japan, on the battlefield. The problem of Jewish civilians in occupied Europe seemed less important. There seemed to be little the United States could do.

But in the spring of 1944, two inmates of Auschwitz escaped the death camp. Newspapers throughout Europe and in the United States reported their stories. People realized there was more to this war than fighting battles. In countries they conquered, the Nazis were carrying out genocide. They were trying to destroy an entire population of Jewish civilians.

In January 1944, President Roosevelt finally decided to take action against Nazi genocide in

Europe. He organized the War Refugee Board. The Board would help rescue people threatened with deportation and the death camps. It would help them escape German-occupied countries and reach safe territory until the end of the war. The War Refugee Board helped Jews in Europe by giving them visas. These documents allowed them to move to the United States and other friendly countries. Members of the Board also threatened Nazi leaders responsible for the persecution. They were warned that after the war, if they survived, they would be put on trial for their crimes.

After German troops occupied Hungary, the War Refugee Board turned its attention to the Hungarian Jews. The Board asked Sweden and other neutral countries, including Switzerland, Spain, and Portugal, to send as many representatives as possible to Budapest. Neutral diplomats would serve as observers and, in any way possible, stop the Nazis from deporting Hungarian Jews. A representative of the War Refugee Board, Ivar

Olsen, was living in Stockholm. The Board asked Olsen to find a capable and courageous Swede, a diplomat who could travel to Budapest and rescue the Jews still living there. Although Hungary was allied to Germany, it allowed neutral Swedish diplomats to live and work in Budapest.

Olsen formed a committee of Swedish Jews. The committee set out plans for the rescue mission and began a search for its leader. Olsen's first choice for the leader was Count Folke Bernadotte, the president of the Swedish Red Cross. But Bernadotte was an important and well-known person. Under pressure from the Germans, the leaders of Hungary refused to allow him into their country.

Finding Wallenberg

Koloman Lauer joined Olsen's committee. Because Lauer was a Hungarian and a Jew, Olsen asked him to take part in the search. On June 9, Lauer told Olsen that he knew

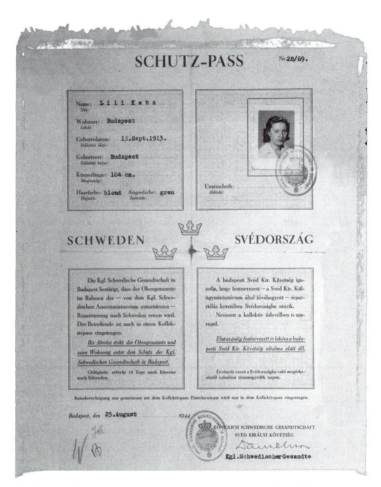

This letter of protection was issued to Lili Katz, a Hungarian Jew, by Raoul Wallenberg on behalf of the War Refugee Board.

just the man to help the War Refugee Board.
This man was a young Swede who could
speak German and several other languages.
Lauer had been impressed by the man's
energy and intelligence and knew he could
carry out this dangerous mission. In fact,
Lauer's choice was one of his own business
colleagues, the thirty-one-year-old salesman
Raoul Wallenberg.

Olsen took Lauer's suggestion. The next
night, Olsen, Lauer, and Wallenberg met to talk
about the mission. It would mean a long trip
through occupied territory. Wallenberg could
expect tiring and frustrating work in a foreign
city and much danger. Nevertheless, Wallenberg
accepted the assignment right away.

The Swedish government, as well as the U.S.
ambassador to Sweden, approved the selection
of Wallenberg for the mission to Budapest. But
Wallenberg set down his own conditions. If
they were not met, he wouldn't take on the job.
He must be able to move about, meet with
whomever he wanted, and act independently

of the Swedish embassy. He wanted to be appointed a first secretary. This was a high official position that would allow him to meet and deal with anyone he wanted, all the way up to the leaders of Hungary.

Wallenberg also wanted as much money as he might need to carry out his mission. He wanted the right to bribe officials whenever it might prove useful. He wanted the authority to buy buildings in Budapest and set up safe houses. He wanted to issue protective passes. The passes would be official Swedish documents and would allow the people holding them to escape arrest and deportation by the Germans or Hungarians.

Wallenberg made many other demands. The leaders of Sweden talked it over. They passed the matter all the way up to the prime minister as well as the Swedish king, Gustav. These officials and the king accepted Wallenberg's conditions.

The leaders of Sweden realized that they should cooperate with Wallenberg and the War

Refugee Board. Although Sweden was neutral, the Swedes opposed Nazism. They also felt some shame for helping Germany early in the war. Sweden had traded its iron ore to Germany, and German factories had used it to make tanks, trucks, guns, and ammunition. Early in the war, Sweden had also allowed the German army to cross its territory to attack the Soviet Union. Now the Swedes wanted to do something to help the other side.

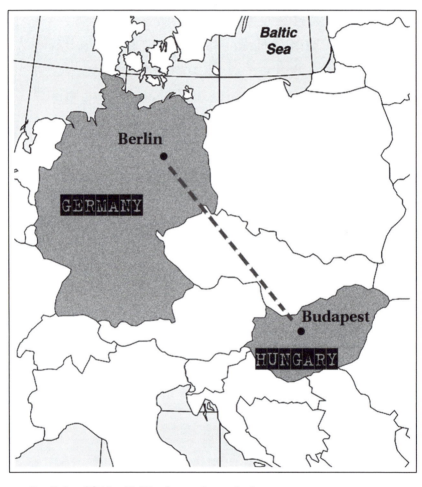

In July 1944, Wallenberg traveled
to Budapest from Berlin.

3. Defying Eichmann

To prepare for his mission, Wallenberg studied newspaper reports from central Europe. He read mail sent by Swedish diplomats already living in Hungary. From the stories and letters, he discovered that the Germans had already sent several hundred thousand Jews out of Hungary to their deaths at Auschwitz and other camps.

Wallenberg realized that he had no time to lose. He left Sweden by plane for Berlin, Germany's capital, on July 6, 1944. In Berlin, he stayed with his half sister Nina, who was married to a Swedish diplomat. Wallenberg felt confident and eager to get to Budapest and get started. He didn't realize that he would never again see Nina, any other member of his family, or his homeland.

It had been exactly one month since the invasion of France by the Allies. Since that time, the Germans had been pushed back in France and on the eastern front. The tide of the war had turned against them. Wallenberg realized that the Nazis would be stepping up their persecution of Jews in occupied territories. They would be rushing to make Hungary and Europe *Judenrein* before the Allies could force their armies back into Germany.

From Berlin, Wallenberg took a passenger train that was carrying German soldiers, who filled the halls and compartments of the train. Unable to find a seat, Wallenberg rested on the floor of a corridor. He carried nothing but the clothes on his back and a knapsack. Inside the knapsack he had packed a change of clothes, a bit of food, a gun, and a list of people in Budapest who might be able to help him. The southbound train passed another train heading north. This train was carrying Hungarian Jews to Poland. On July 9, 1944— the same day Wallenberg arrived in

Budapest—the train's occupants arrived at Auschwitz, where most of them would die.

Life in Budapest

Wallenberg moved into a Swedish diplomatic house. He lived just a few streets from the headquarters of the SS and Adolf Eichmann. But while Wallenberg was eager to start work, Eichmann was angry and frustrated. The leader of Hungary, Miklos Horthy, had just asked the Germans to stop shipping Jews out of his country. The Hungarian police were no longer cooperating with Eichmann's men.

Since March, Eichmann had made progress in Budapest. After his arrival, he had immediately asked the Hungarian government to pass new, stricter laws for Jewish citizens. Fearing that the Germans would take over their government completely, the Hungarians had agreed. All Jews in Budapest had to wear yellow stars that would identify them as

Jewish. They could go outside their homes for only three hours a day. They could not own radios or telephones. The police closed down their businesses and banned them from attending schools, religious services, and public events. The police confiscated bicycles from adults as well as children.

In April 1944, the Hungarian police had begun herding the Jews of Budapest into schools, churches, synagogues, and houses marked with the yellow star. The yellow star made it easy for the police as well as the Germans to find and identify their Jewish targets. The Jews had no choice but to move into these crowded public places, where they often had little food to eat and not even a spot to lie down at night. Under Eichmann's orders, the Budapest Jews had also formed a Jewish council. Eichmann used the council to pass orders and instructions on to the Jewish community. He assured the members of the council that the Jews would be safe as long as they cooperated with him.

Curfews were imposed on Jews in Hungary and
elsewhere in Europe. The sign in the window of
this liquor store reads "Shopping hours for
Jews—3:00 to 5:00 PM" in German and Czech.

Then, in May 1944, the trains began leaving Budapest, packed with Jews and headed for Auschwitz. The overcrowded trains created problems for the Nazis. The commander of Auschwitz, Rudolf Hoess, could not keep up with the thousands of Jews who were arriving at his gates every day. The gas chambers worked overtime, yet the camp was overflowing with new arrivals. Hoess asked Eichmann to slow down the deportations from Hungary, but Eichmann felt determined to finish his job as soon as possible. He asked his own commander, Heinrich Himmler, the chief of the SS, for advice and orders.

The German army desperately needed trains for the transport of its equipment and for its soldiers. In answer to Eichmann, Himmler passed along an order directly from Adolf Hitler. The military could use any trains it wanted, as long as it was advancing. Retreating units would have to walk, if necessary. Since most German troops were now retreating, Eichmann found it easy to get as many trains as he needed. By July 6, the day Raoul Wallenberg left Stockholm, the deportations from the countryside were completed.

For that day, Eichmann had planned a grand roundup of all of the Jews in Budapest. Working together, German soldiers and Hungarian police would march the Jews to an island in the Danube, the river that runs through the middle of the city. From there, they would be sent to the city's train stations for the ride to Auschwitz. But then, Miklos Horthy gave his order stopping the roundup. Just before giving the order, he had sent 1,600 Hungarian policemen out of the city. The Germans needed these men to help them round up the Jews. Even if Eichmann had ignored Horthy's orders, he would not have been able to carry out his plans.

Horthy was a war hero and a Hungarian patriot. At the beginning of World War II, he had decided to cooperate with the Germans. As a reward, Germany had made parts of central Europe Hungarian territory. Hungary had lost this land by a treaty that was signed after World

War I. Horthy admired the German government and felt a strong contempt for the Jews himself. But he also worried about the world's opinion of his country. Germany would probably lose the war. Hungary's future would depend on how much it cooperated with Eichmann and the SS. If the Hungarian leaders helped Eichmann commit his crimes, Horthy knew they would be held responsible by the Allies.

Miklos Horthy ruled Hungary from 1920 to 1944. Though allied with Germany, he parted company with the Nazis over their plan to exterminate the Jews.

Making Passports

After reaching Budapest, Raoul Wallenberg immediately set to work. He set up Section C, a special office within the Swedish embassy. Using money the War Refugee Board had given him, he hired a large new staff. The members of his staff, most of whom were Jewish, prepared special passes for Jewish citizens. Already, the embassy had granted several hundred such passes to those who had business or family connections in Sweden. But only a tiny minority of Jews in Budapest could hope to get such a pass.

Wallenberg now set Section C to work full-time to create new and more official-looking passes. He convinced the Hungarian government to allow him to print 4,500 of them. He helped design the passes and arranged to have them printed on heavy paper. The passes carried photographs and official seals and signatures. The writing stated that the holder would travel to Sweden after

Section C was Raoul Wallenberg's headquarters
in the Swedish embassy in Budapest. This photo
was taken in his office there in November 1944.

the war. Anyone having the pass was protected from being deported, arrested, or harmed in any way. A long line formed every day outside the doors of Section C on Minerva Street. Desperate men and women waited for hours, sometimes days, to receive their protective passes. They knew that the passport might help them to survive Eichmann's next roundup of Jews. The passes might even help them survive the war.

Wallenberg did more than create and sign documents. He hired several hundred Budapest Jews as cooks, drivers, and assistants. He placed their families under the protection of the Swedish embassy. He set up medical clinics, arranged the distribution of food and medicine to Jewish families, and established soup kitchens.

Wallenberg also turned certain large houses in Budapest into safe houses. Again using the money from the War Refugee Board, he arranged to buy these houses from Adolf Eichmann himself. Under Eichmann's orders, the Germans had seized many of these houses from their Jewish owners. Under Wallenberg's direction, the houses now belonged to Sweden, not to Hungary or to the Nazis. Each of them flew the Swedish flag. The flags meant the houses were neutral territory, protected from the police and German troops. They all served the same

In this photo, taken from Wallenberg's car, a group of Jews who have been saved from deportation return from the Josef Varos train station.

purpose—to shelter Jewish families from the Nazis and their northbound trains.

Soon after Wallenberg arrived in Budapest, other neutral embassies—including those of Switzerland, Portugal, and Spain—began imitating his actions. They began issuing their own protective passes and setting up safe houses. Wallenberg worked hard, day and night. He was racing against time. While Section C prepared its special passes, Eichmann was demanding that the deportation of Jews resume.

Running Risks

On August 1, 1944, Raoul Wallenberg met Miklos Horthy. He asked Horthy to expel Eichmann and the SS from Hungary. Two days later, Wallenberg met with the chief of Hungarian police. He also met with several other Hungarian officials. He made demands and gave warnings. He promised that if they continued helping the Nazis to persecute Jews, they would be arrested and put on trial for war crimes when the war ended. The Allies would throw them in prison or execute them. But he, Wallenberg, might be able to help them, if they helped him to protect the Jews.

Wallenberg's threats worked, for a time. But Eichmann also made threats. He surrounded the capital with SS units. He demanded that Horthy allow him to begin deportations again. He asked to deport at least 50,000 more Jews out of the country. He set a new date for this action: August 25. Wallenberg heard about these plans. He wrote a strong letter to the Hungarian government and demanded that the Hungarians stop the deportation. His letter was also signed by ambassadors from Spain, Portugal, and Switzerland. The representative of the pope, the head of the Catholic church, signed as well.

For the time being, the German government did nothing. Then, on August 24, Romania, another German ally, surrendered to the Soviet army. Romania had been an important source of oil for the Germans. Hungary also provided oil. The Germans wanted to keep control of Hungary's oil for the war effort. For now, the easiest way would be to stay friendly with Hungary's leaders. On August 30, Hungary and Germany reached an agreement. Germany would stop the deportations permanently. In exchange, Horthy agreed that the Jews of Budapest would live in camps outside of Budapest, where they had to join forced-labor battalions. The Hungarians did round up groups of Jewish men to dig fortifications and trenches near Budapest. But Hungarian officials dragged their feet on expelling the Jews from the city. For another month, no Jews were sent out of Budapest.

In the meantime, the situation grew worse on the city's streets. Jews going out of doors, at any time of day, ran a very dangerous risk. The members of the Arrow Cross spent their time hunting down, beating, and killing Jews. Thousands of Jewish families searched desperately for an escape, but they found it impossible to leave the city. Police and soldiers blocked the roads and searched the trains. They checked all documents and sent Jews trying to flee back to Budapest. Some Jewish families hid in the homes of Christians who agreed to help them. Others tried to bribe officials for protection. Thousands came to the doors of the Swedish embassy, knowing that Wallenberg's special passports could save their lives.

4. The Baroness

By September 1944, the war was going very badly for the Germans. Romania had surrendered. The Soviet army had reached the border of Hungary and was preparing to attack Budapest. Hungary's leaders realized that the war was lost. They began looking for a way to make peace with the Allies. If Hungary stayed with Germany to the bitter end, the defeat might bring a hostile occupation of their country. They stopped cooperating with Eichmann's actions against the Jews.

For a time, Wallenberg believed the worst was over. Eichmann left the country, and the deportations stopped. Many Jews held protective passes, prepared in Section C of the Swedish embassy. The Hungarian government had agreed to reopen the city's synagogues. Jews were allowed outside their homes all day, like other citizens. Wallenberg cut his staff down to 100. He prepared to end his mission and return home.

Meanwhile, the Soviet army continued its advance. Soviet troops and tanks reached the plains of central Hungary. By the end of September, the Germans had been pushed back even farther. Soviet troops came within fifty miles of Budapest. In early October, on Miklos Horthy's orders, Hungary made a secret agreement with the Soviet Union. Hungary would surrender to the Soviets on October 18. The Germans soon found out about the secret agreement. Suspecting this, Horthy decided to move faster than planned. On October 15—three days earlier than scheduled—he made a radio announcement. Hungary was withdrawing from the war immediately.

Horthy's announcement took many people by surprise—even his own generals in the Hungarian army. These officers were not

By the fall of 1944, Wallenberg was preparing
to leave the Swedish embassy and return home.
His mission appeared to be a success.

prepared to defend Budapest against the Germans and their allies in the Arrow Cross. On the same day, German and Arrow Cross soldiers moved into Budapest. They swarmed into government buildings. To assure Miklos Horthy's cooperation, they kidnapped his son and brought him to a prison camp inside Germany. Miklos Horthy agreed to submit to this coup d'état. He fled Hungary. The leader of the Arrow Cross, Ferenc Szalasi, became the new Hungarian leader.

Arrow Cross soldiers took over radio stations, police stations, and public buildings. Arrow Cross guards took control of the streets. They rounded up Jews, took them into jails and house cellars, and tortured them. They broke into safe houses and forced the occupants out at gunpoint. They killed Jews in cold blood in the streets and along the banks of the Danube.

At his home, Wallenberg learned that Arrow Cross soldiers had broken into his office. He immediately went to the office and

The Arrow Cross took over control
of the Hungarian government in
October 1944.

ordered the soldiers to leave. He then went to
Arrow Cross headquarters and demanded the
release of his driver, who had been arrested.
He spoke loudly and angrily in German.
Unsure of how to deal with this commanding
diplomat, who spoke the language of their
German friends so well, the Arrow Cross
soldiers and officers obeyed him.

The Arrow Cross resumed the deportation
of the Jews and herded others into a
ghetto in the center of Budapest.

Eichmann returned to Budapest the day after the coup. He met with Hungary's new leaders. The Arrow Cross leaders were happy to give their full cooperation. They agreed to begin sending Jews out of Budapest again. Some would be sent to Germany right away as slave laborers. The rest would be brought to concentration camps near Budapest or herded into a ghetto in the middle of the city. The soldiers would seal off the ghetto and prevent anyone from leaving. Slave laborers would build a tall wooden wall, trapping the residents of the ghetto inside.

Eichmann also prepared a final plan to eliminate Budapest's Jewish population. The Arrow Cross and Hungarian police would collect the Jews of the ghetto and the labor camps. They would force the Jews to march to Hungary's border with Austria. There they would be put on trains and sent into Germany. To prevent any more problems or delay, the Arrow Cross announced that they would no longer respect protective passes of any kind.

Wallenberg ordered his staff to make up more protective passes. At first, he had agreed to issue only 4,500 of the passes. Now he decided to make as many as he needed. He would give them freely to anyone that wanted one. He drove around the city, keeping blank passes and a typewriter in his car. Whenever he found someone in trouble with the Germans or the Arrow Cross, he immediately made up a new pass for the person. He climbed out of his car, handed over the pass, and demanded the release of the prisoner. His confident demeanor and his command of German usually brought cooperation from anyone he encountered.

A Beautiful Ally

After the Arrow Cross coup, Wallenberg forgot about returning home to Sweden. Instead, he searched for some new way to resist Eichmann. His passes and safe houses were no longer effective. He needed an ally with close connections to the new government. On October 18, he met that ally—a beautiful young woman named Baroness Elisabeth Kemeny.

The baroness was wealthy and important. She had escaped Austria in 1936 during the *Anschluss,* when Nazi Germany took over her homeland. Like Wallenberg, she came from a famous family. Her new Hungarian husband, Baron Gabor Kemeny, served as the foreign minister in the Arrow Cross government. Although the baroness herself was Jewish, her high status protected her from any harm by the Nazis or the Arrow Cross.

Soon after she married Baron Kemeny, the baroness discovered that he was a Nazi sympathizer and an anti-Semite. The baroness soon felt anger and contempt toward her husband. She also detested Szalasi and the Arrow Cross government. She realized that Hungary had become nothing more than a puppet of Nazi Germany. When she met Wallenberg, she decided to help him in his mission to save the Jews. Wallenberg knew just what the baroness could do. She could persuade her husband to stop the deportations of the Jews. She could demand that his government recognize the protective passports. In return, Wallenberg promised to protect the baron from war crimes trials. These trials were sure to take place after the end of the war. He might save the baron's life. The baroness wanted to spare her husband from a trial and execution after the war. She was already pregnant with her first child. She wanted the child's father to survive the war.

Wallenberg also promised to ask Sweden to officially recognize the Hungarian government. Sweden would agree that Ferenc Szalasi and his ministers were the true rulers of Hungary. To Szalasi, this recognition was even more important than Baron Kemeny's life. Szalasi and the other Arrow Cross leaders sought the world's respect. This respect might come with the formal recognition by Sweden and other nations. The baroness talked to the baron. Baron Kemeny was a proud and devoted member of the Szalasi

Arrow Cross party leader Ferenc Szalasi *(right)*
and his government sought international
recognition of their authority.

government. But he also felt love and devotion toward his young wife. He argued with the baroness, but he finally did as she asked. He persuaded Szalasi to stop the deportations—temporarily.

To carry out this decision, the baron read a proclamation over the radio, while Baroness Kemeny stood at his side. He declared that the soldiers and police would not harm anyone holding protective passes. In addition, Jews no longer had to wear the yellow star. The special houses owned by Sweden and other neutral countries would again be safe from raids. The proclamation did not stop the violence in Budapest, though. The Arrow Cross soldiers were mostly young men. They represented the government in power, and they carried powerful automatic weapons. Few people had the authority or ability to stop them.

Despite Kemeny's proclamation, Arrow Cross men continued to arrest and torture many Jews and shot many others. Every day, they collected thousands of Jews and forced

them to join work battalions. The Jewish
laborers slaved in harsh conditions with no
food or water. Many of them died after just a
few days. The survivors were not allowed to
leave the battalion or return to their homes.
Being forced into a work battalion was a
sentence of death.

Meeting Adolf Eichmann

Every day, Wallenberg showed up in the square
where the roundup of laborers took place. He
ignored the guns and threats of the Arrow
Cross guards. He shouted to the ragged,
hungry, and frightened people in the crowds.
Anyone holding a protective pass, he declared,
should come forward. Anyone who had lost a
pass should also step out of the crowd.

Hundreds of people obeyed Wallenberg's
commands. They stepped out of the crowd,
and away from certain death, even if they
had never held a pass and they had no right
to one. They realized Wallenberg was playing

a trick on their guards. He didn't care if these Jews held passes or not. He didn't care about the rules and regulations set down for the passes. He gave out new passes to anyone who asked for one or who claimed to have lost one.

Meanwhile, Wallenberg made loud protests to the government. He complained about the roundup of slave laborers. He complained about the shootings and torture carried out by the Arrow Cross. He promised that anyone harming Jews would be held responsible for their actions after the war. He sent messages and made phone calls to the highest ministers, even Szalasi himself.

Adolf Eichmann learned about Wallenberg's efforts to frustrate his plans. He grew angry and demanded that Wallenberg come to his office. Wallenberg agreed. His status as a diplomat protected him from the Nazis—or so he thought. The two men met at Eichmann's headquarters in the Majestic Hotel. They talked and argued bitterly. Wallenberg was calm, confident, and persuasive. He claimed that Germany would lose the war, and soon. In reply, Eichmann decided to make an offer. In return for a large sum of money, the Germans would prepare a special train. Some—not all—of the Jews of Budapest could escape Hungary on this train.

Wallenberg promised to think about the offer. But he knew that he would never agree to it. He wouldn't pay the Nazis for the lives of Jews. He also knew that if some Jews were allowed to leave, the ones left behind would probably be killed. After the meeting, Eichmann sent out orders to murder Raoul Wallenberg.

Forced marches of Jewish prisoners, like the one to Hegyashalom, were common in German-occupied Europe.

5. The Final Days of German Occupation

It was November 19, 1944, and Baron Kemeny was furious. Persuaded by his wife, he had helped Raoul Wallenberg stop the deportations of the Jews. Still, Sweden had not recognized the Szalasi government, as Wallenberg had promised. Kemeny sent a message to Wallenberg. If Sweden did not recognize his government by December 14, he would see to it that all the protections for the Jews would end. They would be rounded up. The Arrow Cross and the SS units would kill them immediately or send them to Germany and certain death.

Despite Kemeny's proclamation, Eichmann was again sending Jews out of the city. His victims were forced laborers who were living in camps and factory yards in the outskirts of Budapest. SS and Arrow Cross troops marched their prisoners from these camps all the way to the town of Hegyashalom, on Hungary's border with Austria. The walk took a full week, at the rate of twenty miles a day. The marchers had no food, no water, and no shelter. Along the way, thousands died of starvation, sickness, and exposure to the cold. Many others became too tired or sick to continue walking. Arrow Cross soldiers followed along, shooting anyone sitting or lying by the road. By the time the columns reached Hegyashalom, most of the people that had started out were already dead. At the border town of Hegyashalom, SS guards placed the survivors on trains. The trains brought them into Austria and then Germany.

Wallenberg heard about the forced march to Hegyashalom. He drove out along the long columns of marchers. He delivered food and water where he could, and he rescued those marchers holding protective passes. He made loud protests to the guards and their officers along the road. He managed to stop hundreds of murders.

Hungarian Arrow Cross soldiers supervise the
loading of a deportation train.

On November 23, Wallenberg drove all the
way to Hegyashalom. He reached the train
station with a few members of his staff. The SS
guards did not stop him. Although they had
lost the war and the Soviets were advancing,
they still respected him as a neutral diplomat.
Wallenberg ordered the guards to stand aside
and allow him to find people holding
protective passes. Hundreds of people already

on the trains climbed out. Wallenberg began shouting out names. He used any common names that came to mind. He demanded that the named people come forward. Hundreds escaped the train, climbed onto waiting trucks, and returned to Budapest. Before Wallenberg left Hegyashalom that day, he unloaded a truckload of food. He asked the guards to give the food to the Jews still on the trains. It was all he could do for them.

Fleeing the City

By the end of November, as the Soviet army approached, the city of Budapest was in chaos. Thousands of people fled the city. They packed into cars and trains and fled to the west, away from the Soviet soldiers. They knew that the Germans would fight for the city and that a terrible battle was about to take place.

Arrow Cross patrols roamed the city. They searched out Jewish citizens in the streets

As the Soviet army approached Budapest, thousands
fled the city and chaos reigned. The ruins of a
Jewish youth center are pictured above.

and houses. As soon as they discovered a Jewish person, they began robbing and beating him or her. They led their victims into jails, where they tortured them for hours before killing them. They also marched hundreds of Jews to the banks of the Danube. They shot their victims as soon as they reached the river. To save bullets, they tied two or three victims together. They killed one prisoner and then shoved all of them into the freezing water. The living were dragged down into the river by the dead.

Wallenberg could do little to stop these acts. He realized by now that his own life was in danger. There were orders out to kill him, by any means possible. His status as a diplomat would no longer protect him. One day, a German truck smashed into his car. Wallenberg realized that it wasn't an accident. Luckily, he had not been inside the car at the time. While diplomats of Sweden and other countries prepared their escape from Budapest, Wallenberg continued working, night and day, to save the Jews.

On November 29, Baroness Kemeny also prepared to leave. She was under suspicion for helping Wallenberg. One Arrow Cross official ordered her to be arrested. President Szalasi himself stopped the arrest. He demanded that she leave the country within one day. The baroness packed her bags and boarded a train for Italy. At the station to bid her farewell was Raoul Wallenberg. He and the baroness had become close friends. But now they were parting for good. They would never meet again.

The Final Days

In December, Adolf Eichmann ordered the remaining Jews of Budapest to be collected into the ghetto. The police and the Arrow Cross jammed thousands of Jews into houses and apartments. Crowds of hungry, desperate people lived in hallways, on staircases, and in basements. Others were not lucky enough to even have a roof over their heads. They lived in the streets and slept on the sidewalks.

In the middle of December 1944, the Arrow Cross leaders of Hungary fled Budapest. On December 22, Adolf Eichmann also fled, along with the SS soldiers under his command. On the day after Christmas, the Soviets surrounded the city and blocked all roads and railroad lines.

Law and order came to an end in Budapest. Arrow Cross gangs roamed through the city, killing, robbing, and beating. Thousands of people were brought to torture chambers or to the banks of the Danube for execution. The Arrow Cross raided homes and hospitals. Young children and sick elderly patients were murdered on the spot or marched to the river.

Wallenberg continued issuing protective passes, sheltering Jews in safe houses, distributing food, and making protests to the Arrow Cross leaders who remained in the city. He bribed soldiers and policemen to prevent further roundups of Jews on the streets. He hid people in basements, attics, and even in the underground vault of a bank. Several times, he also stopped the Arrow Cross from herding more Jews into the crammed ghetto, where thousands of people were starving to death. In addition, he bribed regular Hungarian policemen to bring people out of the ghetto and to a safe house.

As the Soviet army drew closer to Budapest, the city grew more dangerous for Wallenberg. Nobody was safe, not even those who worked for the Swedish embassy. On January 7, Arrow Cross men attacked a safe house on Jokai Street that Wallenberg had set up. Neither the protective passes nor the Swedish flag flying over the house protected the inhabitants. Nearly 300 people were taken out of the house, beaten, and marched away. The Arrow Cross forced many of their captives into work brigades. Within a few days, most of these laborers were murdered.

Knowing that the city would soon fall, the Germans and the Arrow Cross prepared to kill all the people who remained inside the ghetto. SS officers drew up the plans. A machine-gun unit would assemble at the entrance to the ghetto. They would march inside and gun down the 70,000 Jews still living within the ghetto walls.

As Soviet units advanced from the north, a friend of Wallenberg's, Pal Szalai, learned about the mass murder that would soon take place in the ghetto. Szalai was determined to stop it. He rushed to the Royal Hotel, where German soldiers, Arrow Cross units, and Hungarian policemen were gathering and preparing to take part in the massacre. Inside the hotel, Szalai found an SS general named Schmidthuber. Szalai gave Schmidthuber a warning from Wallenberg. If the ghetto massacre took place, the general would be held personally responsible for it. He would be put on trial and probably executed as a war criminal.

After listening to Szalai, Schmidthuber immediately called off the massacre. He ordered the Germans and Arrow Cross to stay away from the ghetto. Even though Wallenberg was not present, his threats prevented the murder of thousands of Jews in the ghetto. In all, 120,000 Jews were still living in Budapest. They made up more than half of the total Jewish population of the city before the war. Most of them had Raoul Wallenberg to thank for their survival.

6. A Prisoner of the Soviets

It was the second week of January 1945. The battle for Budapest raged. German and Hungarian troops fought desperately in the streets. Tanks rumbled over barricades and trenches. Heavy Soviet guns shelled the city night and day. The fighting and killing continued from one house to the next. To avoid the bloody street fighting, thousands of Soviet soldiers advanced through underground tunnels and cellars toward the center of Budapest.

On January 10, Wallenberg drove to German army headquarters. He asked the Germans not to attack the safe houses where Jews and members of the Swedish embassy were now hiding from the fighting. On the next day, he finally took shelter in the cellar of a house on Benczur Street. The house was under the protection of the International Red Cross. Wallenberg knew that the house lay directly in the path of the advancing Soviet soldiers. He moved to Benczur Street because he wanted to meet the Soviets as soon as possible. Wallenberg knew that the fighting would soon end. The Germans would retreat and the Soviets would win the battle for Budapest. He wanted the Soviets to help him get desperately needed food and medicine into the city after the fighting ended. He also wanted their support for his plans for the Hungarian Jews.

While running all over Budapest and saving thousands of lives, Wallenberg had been working on a new plan. After the war, he would set up the Wallenberg Institute for Support and Reconstruction. This organization would help Jews reunite with their families. It would provide them with money, food, and housing if needed. It would help them find jobs. It would also help Jews who wanted to emigrate to Palestine, where Wallenberg expected a new Jewish homeland to be established. The Institute would use money from the U.S. War Refugee Board that was still available to Wallenberg. He would also raise money from wealthy Hungarians, from Swedes, and from anybody who had the ability to contribute.

On January 13, the Soviet army reached the house on Benczur Street. Major Dimitri Demchinkov arrived to talk to Raoul Wallenberg. Demchinkov took Wallenberg and his driver, Vilmos Langfelder, to his headquarters. There Wallenberg asked permission to travel to the city of Debrecen, where the leader of the Soviet army directed the battle for Hungary. The NKVD, or Soviet secret police, then took Wallenberg into custody. They questioned him for three days about his actions in Budapest. They allowed him to move around the city freely. But a three-man escort followed him everywhere he went.

Already, most of the employees of the Swedish embassy had escaped Hungary. The Soviets could not understand why Raoul Wallenberg had remained behind. They suspected that Wallenberg was some kind of spy. There seemed no good reason for him to stay in this dangerous city when nearly everyone who could leave had done so long ago.

The Prisoner

On January 17, Wallenberg prepared to leave Budapest. Scattered fighting was still taking place in the city and in the surrounding countryside. But instead of returning to Sweden and safety, Wallenberg and his driver, Vilmos Langfelder, planned to drive to Debrecen. The Soviet commander, Marshal Malinovsky, had his headquarters there, and a group of Hungarians had formed a government. This government would be friendly to the Soviet Union. Its members would take power in Hungary after the war, under the watchful guidance of Soviet officers and troops.

Wallenberg wanted to meet Malinovsky and ask him to protect the Jews. He also wanted to persuade Malinovsky to help his postwar relief effort. He expected to return to Budapest after the meeting with Malinovsky. He had been dealing with the Nazis and their Hungarian allies since July 1944. He felt certain that he could also deal with the Soviets and that he could persuade them to cooperate with him. After all, the diplomats of Sweden had protected Soviet property in Budapest during the war. If necessary, Wallenberg would offer Malinovsky a bribe. He brought a large amount of money with him. He also ordered his driver to hide gold and jewelry in the gas tank of his car. These valuables had been given to him for safekeeping by Jewish and Christian families of Budapest.

Outside of Budapest, a group of Soviet NKVD agents stopped Wallenberg's car. They ordered Wallenberg and Langfelder out of the car and arrested them. They brought the two men to Debrecen. Wallenberg still expected to meet Marshal Malinovsky. The meeting did not take place. Instead, the NKVD put Wallenberg and Langfelder on an eastbound train. For two weeks, the train proceeded through eastern Europe, through Romania, the Ukraine, and Russia. Finally, on January 31, 1945, it reached Moscow, the capital of the Soviet Union.

The Soviet police brought Wallenberg and Langfelder to the Lubyanka, a huge prison and police headquarters in central Moscow. Here the NKVD held and interrogated thousands of prisoners. Many of them were foreigners like Wallenberg. They were Austrians, Germans, Italians, Swiss, even a few Americans. The Soviets accused these prisoners of being spies. Most of them would be released after the end of the war.

Wallenberg and Langfelder were separated and placed in small prison cells. Wallenberg remained at the Lubyanka for three months, until April 1945. There he met several other prisoners who had been captured by the Soviets in Europe. He patiently waited for his freedom, believing there had been a misunderstanding, or just a mistake. He wasn't a spy, and he had never worked against the Soviet Union. He believed that he would win his release and return to Sweden after the end of the war.

Questions and Answers

Meanwhile, the war went on in Hungary. Soviet and German soldiers fought in Budapest until the end of February 1945. Soviet control did not bring safety to the people of the city. Soviet soldiers broke into houses, beating the inhabitants and stealing money and valuables. There was little food, and thousands of people were starving.

Wallenberg's family feared for his safety. A story about Wallenberg appeared in a leading Swedish newspaper. For the first time, the people of Sweden learned who Raoul Wallenberg was and what he had done during the war. Swedish leaders began asking questions about Wallenberg. Where was he? Why had the Soviets brought him back to the Soviet Union? When would they release him?

Soviet officials answered these questions. They reported that Wallenberg was safe and in custody. Alexandra Kollontai, the Soviet ambassador to Sweden, told Maj von Dardel, Wallenberg's mother, that he would soon return. But Wallenberg was not released. In April 1945, the NKVD moved him from the Lubyanka to the Lefortovo prison in another part of Moscow. There he went through several long interrogations. Prison officials asked him many questions about his activities in Budapest. Wallenberg would stay in Lefortovo prison for two more years.

The war in Europe ended in May 1945. The war between the United States and Japan ended in August. But the end of the fighting did not bring Raoul Wallenberg his freedom.

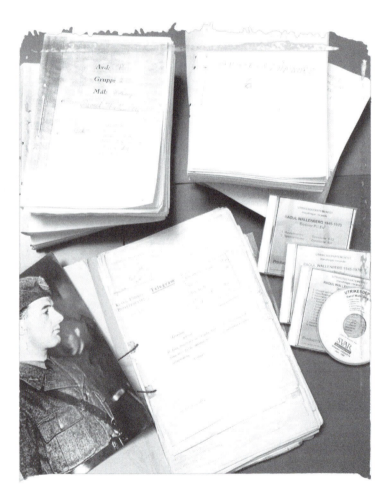

This collection of previously
secret documents on Wallenberg
was released by Sweden in 1997.

The Soviets did not release him from prison. They did not believe his stories and explanations. Wallenberg, a member of a rich Swedish family, would never live in a dangerous place like Budapest and spend his time saving Jews, or so they thought. Wallenberg must have been up to something very different during the war. His position as a Swedish diplomat was just a trick, a cover for a very different job.

The Cold War

The Soviets believed that the Germans were using Wallenberg as a spy. If not the Germans, then the Americans. Although the United States and the Soviet Union were allies during the war, they were also rivals with very different political and economic systems. After World War II, they would become the world's two most powerful nations. These two superpowers would fight the Cold War around the world. Wallenberg, because he had once lived in the United States, came under suspicion. By interrogating Wallenberg's friends after the war, Soviet officials also learned that he had been hired by the War Refugee Board, an agency of the United States government. In the eyes of Soviet officials, this made him their enemy.

While Wallenberg lived, slept, read, and ate in a tiny jail cell, the Soviet army occupied Hungary. The Soviets saw to it that Hungary, and several other central European nations, would ally with the Soviet Union after the war. These nations would adopt the Soviet system of government. They would allow Soviet troops to remain within their borders. They would protect the Soviet Union from attack by western European nations allied to the United States.

Wallenberg did not give up. He wrote many letters and petitions to Soviet officials. He wrote one to Josef Stalin, the leader of the Soviet Union. He received no replies. He asked to see a Swedish diplomat, or a member of the Red Cross. The prison officials refused. They felt certain of his guilt. After all, nobody from Sweden was demanding his release. The Soviets did not bother to put Wallenberg on trial. They did not sentence him for a crime or pass a prison sentence. They simply kept him prisoner.

The one Swede who might have been able to help Wallenberg was Steffan Soderblom. He served as Sweden's ambassador to the Soviet Union. At first, Soderblom believed that Wallenberg was dead. He did not press the Soviet government for any further information. Then the U. S. ambassador, Averill Harriman, offered to help. Certainly the Soviet Union would pay attention to a U. S. ambassador, representing a much more powerful country than Sweden. But Soderblom turned down Harriman's offer of help.

In June 1946, Soderblom met with Josef Stalin. He mentioned Wallenberg to Stalin. But he also said that Wallenberg was probably dead. Stalin promised to help by finding out about Wallenberg himself. He was the most

In 1946, Josef Stalin promised Steffan Soderblom, Sweden's ambassador to the Soviet Union, that he would help to find Wallenberg.

powerful man in the Soviet Union and he was feared by everyone. But after the meeting with Soderblom, Stalin did nothing.

In April 1947, prison guards took Wallenberg out of his cell at Lefortovo prison. They placed him on a train. Most of the other prisoners were Soviet citizens. They had been arrested for political crimes. They had spoken out against the Soviet government or were suspected of opposing Stalin. Wallenberg, like them, was a political prisoner. The entire group was sent to Vorkuta, a prison camp in Siberia, the coldest and most remote region of the Soviet Union.

One Young Diplomat

In the meantime, Wallenberg's family was still trying to free him from the Soviet Union. His mother, Maj von Dardel, made many phone calls and wrote many letters to Swedish officials. But the many questions about Wallenberg began to anger Soviet officials.

97

Finally, on August 18, 1947, a Soviet official named Andrei Vyshinsky made a statement. He claimed that Wallenberg had never been in the Soviet Union. He also claimed there were no records of Wallenberg. Vyshinsky said Wallenberg had probably died at the hands of German or Hungarian Nazis during the fighting for Hungary.

The new government of Hungary also replied to questions and letters about Wallenberg. The Hungarian leaders claimed that Wallenberg had been killed on January 17, 1945, the day he had set out for Debrecen with Vilmos Langfelder.

Sweden did not press the matter of Raoul Wallenberg. Compared to the Soviet Union, Sweden was a small and very weak country. The Swedes did not want to anger Soviet officials. After all, millions of people had died during the war. Millions more were missing and probably dead. Wallenberg might be one of them. One young diplomat, no matter what he had done to help the Jews of Budapest, did not seem worth all the trouble.

The people of Sweden did not forget about Raoul Wallenberg. Newspaper articles, radio reports, and books reminded them about his deeds in Budapest. The writer who did the most to remind them was Rudolf Philipp. He was a Jew from Austria who had escaped to Sweden when Nazi Germany took over Austria. In 1946, Philipp wrote a book about Wallenberg. In the book, he told the story of Wallenberg's heroism in Budapest. He also claimed that Wallenberg was still alive, somewhere in the Soviet Union.

Philipp's book won a large audience in Sweden. He convinced many Swedes to continue asking questions about their missing diplomat. A special committee was formed, called the Wallenberg Committee. The committee pressured the Swedish government to take action to find and return Wallenberg.

Meanwhile, in the Soviet Union, Wallenberg continued to be moved from one prison to the next. In 1951, he was moved to a prison camp in Verkhneuralsk. Two years later, Wallenberg was moved again, to a large prison in the city of Vladimir. In the Vladimir prison, Wallenberg was placed in a cell with one other prisoner, a Russian. He was not allowed to see or talk to any other prisoners. Once a day the guards marched him to a small exercise cell, where he exercised alone under their watchful eyes.

Wallenberg was not allowed to receive any letters or food from the outside world. Soviet officials did not want anyone getting the word out that Wallenberg was still alive. They did not want the rest of the world to know that Wallenberg was still their prisoner. They did not want to admit they had made a mistake. Anyone who met and recognized Wallenberg was immediately sent to a different prison.

On February 6, 1957, the Soviet government finally made a direct answer to the many appeals made for information on Raoul Wallenberg. An official memorandum declared that on July 17, 1947, A. L. Smoltsov,

This monument to Raoul Wallenberg was unveiled
in May 1999 in the Stockholm suburb of
Lidingo, where he was born.

the head of the prison hospital service, reported that Raoul Wallenberg had died suddenly the night before of a heart attack. From that time on, the Soviets made the same answer every time they were asked about Raoul Wallenberg. According to their records, he had died of a heart attack in 1947. Few people outside the Soviet Union believed this. Many Soviet prisoners claimed to have met Wallenberg, either in a jail cell or during transportation from one prison to the next. Their reports appeared in books and newspaper stories.

The Cold War between the United States and the Soviet Union dragged on. The two superpowers were fighting for allies in Europe, Africa, and Asia. The imprisonment of one man seemed to matter very little. Sweden and the United States demanded information, but when Soviet officials refused to give it, the matter was dropped.

In the fall of 1980, the United States Congress made Raoul Wallenberg an honorary U.S. citizen. The people of Budapest raised a memorial in honor of Wallenberg and his mission to their city, and named a street after him.

In 1990, the Soviet government fell from power. A new government took its place. Still, Raoul Wallenberg did not appear. The new government gave out no new information about him. If he was alive, he would have been seventy-eight years old and would have spent forty-five years in Soviet prisons. If he was dead, there were no reliable reports about when or how he had died, or where he was buried.

After spending a few dangerous months saving thousands of people from death at the hands of the Nazis, Raoul Wallenberg had disappeared, a prisoner of the Soviet government and a victim of the Cold War. Nevertheless, his name and his deeds survived. Today he is remembered throughout the world as one of the heroes of World War II.

Timeline

August 4, 1912	Raoul Wallenberg is born.
1931	Wallenberg journeys to the United States and enrolls at the University of Michigan.
1935	His grandfather sends Wallenberg to South Africa to become a businessman.
1939	Germany attacks Poland, beginning World War II.
1940	Wallenberg goes to work as a salesman for the Central European Trading Company.
1941	Wallenberg travels and witnesses the Nazi occupation of Europe.
January 1944	President Roosevelt establishes the War Refugee Board to help those fleeing Nazi-occupied countries.
March 1944	German troops invade Hungary.

May 1944	Deportation of Hungarian Jews to Auschwitz begins.
July 1944	Wallenberg arrives in Budapest.
October 1944	The Hungarian government tries to sever ties with the Nazis and is overthrown by fascist extremists.
December 1944	Eichmann and his SS troops flee Budapest as Soviet troops surround the city.
January 1945	Soviet troops enter Budapest. Soviet secret police arrest Wallenberg. He is never heard from again.

Glossary

Allies
The group of countries fighting the Axis powers of Germany and Japan during World War II. The United States, Great Britain, France, and the Soviet Union all belonged to the Allies.

Anschluss
The invasion of Austria and overthrow of the Austrian government by Nazi Germany in 1936.

anti-Semite
An individual who fears and hates Jewish people and the Jewish religion.

Arrow Cross (Nyilas)
A Hungarian political party closely allied with the Nazi Party of Germany.

Auschwitz
A prison camp set up by the Germans in southern Poland during World War II. The Germans gathered civilians from all over central Europe and sent them to Auschwitz to be murdered.

Axis
A word indicating Nazi Germany and its allies
during World War II.

Cold War
The worldwide rivalry between the United States
and the Soviet Union that began after their
common victory over Nazi Germany in World
War II.

coup d'état
The sudden overthrow of an established
government by its opponents.

Enskilda Bank
A private Swedish bank owned by the
Wallenberg family.

ghetto
During World War II, a neighborhood forcibly set
up by Nazi occupation forces for Jewish citizens.

Jewish council
A committee of leading Jewish citizens, set up and
controlled by Nazi occupation forces in order to
control Jewish civilians.

Judenrein
A German word meaning "free of Jews." It was the
goal of Nazi Germany to make all areas
occupied by its armies *Judenrein*.

Nazi Party
A political party led by Adolf Hitler that took power in Germany in 1933.

NKVD
The secret police force of the Soviet Union, used to arrest and imprison Soviet enemies during World War II.

Schutzstaffel (SS)
A special branch of the military services of Nazi Germany. The SS dealt with the control and persecution of people living under Nazi occupation, especially the Jews.

Section C
A special department of the Swedish embassy in Budapest, Hungary. Raoul Wallenberg used Section C to issue protective passes and assist Hungary's Jews.

Wallenberg Committee
A board of Swedish citizens set up to search for Raoul Wallenberg after his disappearance.

War Refugee Board
A department of the United States federal government, set up to protect persecuted civilians in Europe during World War II.

For More Information

Jewish Student Online Research Center (JSOURCE)
http://www.us-israel.org/
jsource/biography/wallenberg.html

Raoul Wallenberg
http://www.geocities.com/Athens/Academy/2393/

The Raoul Wallenberg Project Interviews
Uppsala University
http://rwa.bibks.uu.se/

The Simon Wiesenthal Center
http://www.wiesenthal.com/resource/gloss.htm

Yad Vashem
http://www.yadvashem.org.il/yadvashem/visit/
trees/wallenberg.html

For Further Reading

Bierman, John. *Righteous Gentile: The Story of Raoul Wallenberg, Missing Hero of the Holocaust.* New York: Penguin Books, 1995.

Lester, Elenore. *Wallenberg: The Man in the Iron Web.* Englewood Cliffs, NJ: Prentice-Hall, Inc., 1982.

Linnea, Sharon. *Raoul Wallenberg: The Man Who Stopped Death.* Philadelphia: Jewish Publication Society, 1993.

Werbell, Frederick E., and Thurston Clarke. *Lost Hero: The Mystery of Raoul Wallenberg.* New York: McGraw-Hill Book Company, 1982.

Index

About the Author

Tom Streissguth was born in Washington, DC, and raised in Minneapolis. He has traveled widely in Europe and the Middle East and has worked as an editor, journalist, and teacher. In 1999, he cofounded a summer language school in St. Leger-en-Bray, a village in northern France. He has written more than forty nonfiction books, including biography, geography, and history, for young readers.

Photo Credits

Cover image © Thomas Veres/United States Holocaust Memorial Museum (USHMM); pp. 6, 50, 52, 59, 62 © Thomas Veres/USHMM; pp. 9, 48, 75 © Yad Vashem Photo Archives/USHMM; p. 13 © Hagstromer & Qviberg Fondkommission AB/USHMM; p. 16 © Erich C. Jochberg/USHMM; p. 18 © William Gallagher/USHMM; pp. 20, 26, 30, 45, 67 © USHMM; p. 22 © National Archives/USHMM; p. 29 © Archiwum Dokumentocji Mechanizney; p. 36 © Lena Kurtz Deutsch/USHMM; p. 61 © Eva Hevesi Ehrlich/USHMM; p. 72 © Ivan Sved/USHMM; p. 77 © Magyar Zsido Museum es Leveltar/USHMM; p. 92 © Jonas Ekstromer/AP/Worldwide; p. 96 © AP/Worldwide; p. 101© Bertil Ericson/AP/Worldwide.

Layout

Geri Giordano

Series Design

Cindy Williamson